SEE INSIDE
AN ANCIENT CHINESE TOWN

SERIES EDITOR **R.J. UNSTEAD**

KINGFISHER BOOKS

Series Editor
R. J. Unstead

Author
Penelope Hughes-Stanton

Adviser
Robert Knox

Illustrators
Charlotte Snook, Mike Saunders,
Rob McCaig

This revised edition published in 1986 by
Kingfisher Books Limited, Elsley Court,
20–22 Great Titchfield Street, London W1P 7AD
A Grisewood & Dempsey Company
Originally published in hardcover by
Hutchinson & Co (Publishers) Limited in 1979.
BRITISH LIBRARY CATALOGUING IN PUBLICATION DATA
Hughes-Stanton, Penelope
   See inside an ancient Chinese town.—2nd ed.–(See inside)
   1. City and town life—China—History—
Juvenile literature   2. China—Social life and
customs—221 BC–960 AD—Juvenile literature
   3. Loyang (China)—Social life and customs–
I. Title
931   DS747.42
ISBN 0-86272-203-9
Printed in Hong Kong

CONTENTS

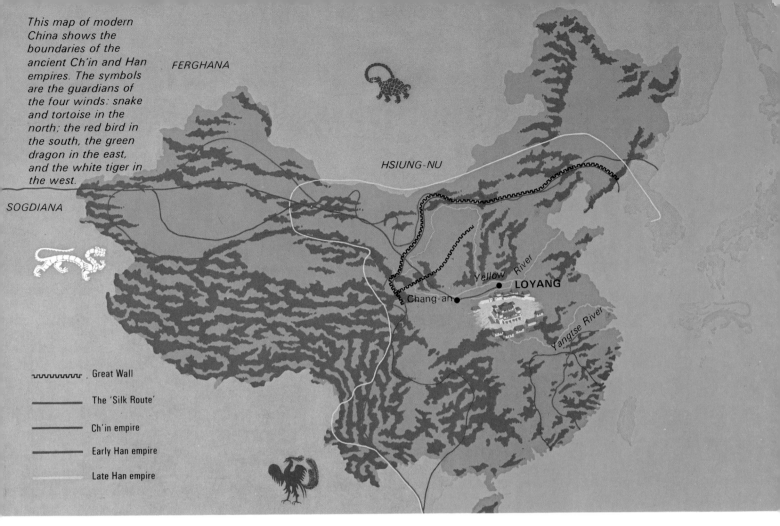

This map of modern China shows the boundaries of the ancient Ch'in and Han empires. The symbols are the guardians of the four winds: snake and tortoise in the north; the red bird in the south, the green dragon in the east, and the white tiger in the west.

FERGHANA

SOGDIANA

HSIUNG-NU

Yellow River
Chang-an
LOYANG
Yangtse River

〰〰〰 Great Wall

──── The 'Silk Route'

──── Ch'in empire

──── Early Han empire

──── Late Han empire

Early China

In AD 25 Loyang became the new capital of the Han empire of China. Ch'ang-an, the old capital, had been destroyed during an uprising. Now, with order restored, Loyang was the centre of a civilization that was already highly advanced and which was hardly to change until the present century.

Loyang was built on a tributary of the mighty Yellow River, the cradle of Chinese civilization. People have lived in the river valley for over half a million years. Prehistoric men, of a type known as Peking Man, hunted there for elephants and deer. Then about 4000 years ago, the people of north China learned to farm and so settled in villages. In time, the villages prospered and grew into towns.

The first dynasty (ruling family) about which we know anything very much was the Shang (1500 BC – 1100 BC). Their society was well organized. They had a system of writing and knew how to cast bronze. The emperors governed through a feudal system: the empire was divided into districts governed by loyal rulers who promised to send men to fight for the emperor in return for protection.

In about 1100 BC the Shang were overthrown by the Chou. But the Chou gradually lost control of the district lords and fighting broke out. The 'Warring States' period that followed ended with the victory of the small state of Ch'in. The empire was united, but so harsh was the emperor's rule that, when he died, rebellions raged and the dynasty collapsed.

In 206 BC a peasant leader founded the Han dynasty; and peace was restored. The emperor ruled through officials who were sent to all parts of the empire. After a rebellion in which the capital Ch'ang-an was sacked, the dynasty was to last for 200 years with Loyang as its capital.

Opposite: Bronze models of the massed cavalry that went on the great military expeditions to defend and enlarge the empire.

3

The Town of Loyang

Loyang occupies a strip of land between the Mang Mountains and the Lo River, from which it takes its name. It lies about 25 kilometres (15 miles) east of modern Loyang. Both river and mountain form good natural protection, but for extra defence a 20 metre-wide (22 yards) stamped earth wall and moat have been built round the town.

You enter the town through one of the gates, some of which are as high as 30 metres (33 yards) and serve as watch towers. The town is laid out on a rectangular pattern, north-south roads being crossed by east-west roads. The square zones formed by this criss-crossing are known as 'wards'. Each ward is walled and has its own gate, which is closed at night.

The most impressive part of the town is the emperor's palace in the north. It, too, is surrounded by a high wall with massive towered gates wide enough to let carriages through three abreast. The finest houses in the town are to be found near the palace. The poorest people live in the crowded streets near the market places and main gates.

This road is the start of the 'silk route' to the west. It leads first to Ch'ang-an, the old capital of the Han empire. From Ch'ang-an, merchants continued their journey across mountains and deserts with silks for the Romans; along the road soldiers marched to keep watch on the Great Wall.

Ron Jobson

To the north, inside the walls of the town, is the burial ground of royalty and officials. The burial mounds you can see are known as tumuli.

Loyang lies between the Mang Mountains and the Lo River. It faces south and is rectangular in shape, measuring two kilometres by three kilometres (one mile by two miles). The town is divided into 'wards'. The northern area is occupied by the imperial palace with its granary, stables, temples and pleasure gardens.

A Rich Man's House

This is a house in which an important official in Loyang might have lived. It is surrounded by a wall for privacy. To reach the house itself, you enter through the main gate and cross two courtyards.

The wooden pillars and beams which form the main structure of the house are gaily painted and lacquered (see page 7). The plastered walls of the house are painted with geometric designs. The roofs and tops of the walls are covered with semi-circular pottery tiles. The roof ends are finished off with round tiles decorated with fabulous beasts.

Built into one of the walls is a watchtower from which guards at night keep a constant look out for intruders. In the daytime the women and children sometimes climb the tower to watch the town below.

As you pass into the second courtyard there is a long building on the left. It contains bedrooms and two private sitting rooms, a large one for the master and a smaller one for his wife. In the building straight ahead of you a banquet is taking place. The guests sit on the floor on fur rugs, mats and large colourful cushions. The rooms are richly decorated with silk hangings, painted screens and large bronze urns full of dried flowers. We know the type of houses people lived in from models and pictures found in tombs of this period.

Very rich people might live in houses with three or even four storeys and many more courtyards, some with beautiful willows, pine trees and fishponds full of golden carp.

The poor live in narrow crowded streets in cramped shacks with dried mud walls and thatched roofs. In winter they cover the windows with hemp curtains and wrap themselves in thick quilts.

Below: Notice the tiled roofs and the tops of the walls, and also how everything looks inwards.

The poorer families of Loyang live crammed together in homes like this one. The roof is thatched and the walls are made of mud plaster.

Bottom: In the courtyard under the watchtower there is a pigsty. A servant leads a pig to the kitchen on the left where the banquet is being prepared. Other servants carry dishes into the house. In small houses the kitchen might be inside the main building, but here the smell, noise, and dirt are kept well away.

Below: Here you can see the rich furnishings inside the house. The official must be very important to have two guards at the door. On arrival guests leave their chariots in the front courtyard.

7

Clothes and Food

The clothes of rich people in Loyang are made of fine silk, often embroidered with complicated patterns. In winter they wear padded clothes and rich furs of badger and beaver.

At court and at religious ceremonies there are strict rules of dress. The shape of the hat, the colour of the robe and the symbols embroidered on it all help to show a person's rank. Yellow, for instance, is worn only by the imperial family; and at weddings the more important you are, the more colourful your clothes can be.

As you can see from the banquet scenes (above), the clothes for men and women are much the same: a floor-length, long-

Above: Men and women guests are entertained in different rooms by the host and his lady. They sit on the floor on mats or on little stools. Notice the similarity between the men and women's rich silk robes.

Right: The kitchen, where a banquet is being prepared, is a hive of activity. The rich eat lavishly. Delicacies include turtle, game and dog. A bowl of millet always forms part of the meal. Chopsticks are used to eat with.

sleeved silken robe wrapped round the body and kept in place by a belt or sash.

Men tie their hair up in a knot and cover it with a cloth and hat. (People only cut their hair when in mourning.) Women pile up their hair and decorate it with pins and jewellery. They also wear earrings, bracelets and beautiful belt-hooks. Shoes are made of silk and have wooden soles.

Poor people wear simple tunics made of hemp, tied at the waist. On their feet they wear straw sandals.

The rich of Loyang eat lavishly. They start with a *keng* (stew) of ox, mutton, deer, pig or even dog. This is followed by such exotic dishes as bear's paw, baked owl or panther's breast! Favourite vegetables include bamboo shoots and lotus roots. The meal ends with a bowl of grain food, usually millet, and fruit. Wine, made from grain, is drunk in great quantities.

For the poor there is no such luxury. Most people live on vegetable *keng* and a bowl of millet. Only rarely do they eat meat. From beans and wheat they make bean-curd, noodles and steamed buns.

Above: Fine example of Han dynasty belt-hooks, one in the shape of a tiger, the other of a bird inlaid with turquoise. At first belt-hooks were part of a warrior's outfit; later they were worn everyday, but mostly by men.

Great Inventors

The emperor's palace and the wealthy houses of Loyang are filled with the fine works of potters, stone-carvers, silk-weavers and lacquer workers. Thousands of skilled craftsmen are needed to provide every kind of luxury from beautiful mirrors with elaborate patterns on the back to bronze vessels and bells, carved jades and delicately shaped and gaily painted pottery.

As well as craftsmen and artists, the empire boasts skilled technicians and inventors, far ahead of their time and rivals. The large picture on the right shows paper being made (paper is one of the great discoveries of the Han dynasty). The raw material is hemp, old silk or mulberry bark. These are things that are easy to get hold of, so making paper is very cheap.

Two of the main industries of the empire are the production of salt and iron. Both are controlled by the government, so as to prevent merchants making large profits from these vital products. Salt is essential to those who live on a grain-based diet, and tools made of iron make life on the land much easier. Also they gave employment to thousands of peasants.

In iron-making large piston bellows are used to increase the heat in the blast furnaces which melt the ore. The molten ore is cast in moulds. (It is to be another 1800 years before cast iron is made in Europe.) It is with the tools made from iron that the craftsmen fashion their beautiful objects.

During this Han period there are a number of brilliant physicians who have learnt to diagnose and treat diseases, some with herbal medicines; others by *acupuncture*. In acupuncture fine needles are put in certain parts of the human body to control pain. How acupuncture cures ailments remains a mystery, but in China today it is still considered the most effective way to heal people.

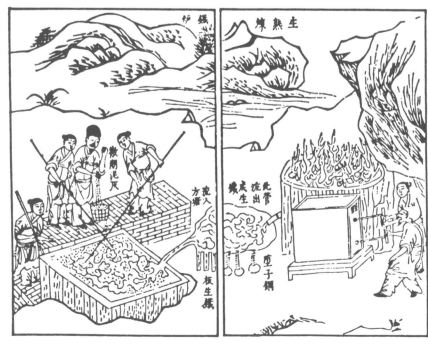

Left: Paper-making – one of the many technical achievements of the Han dynasty. The picture shows different stages in the process: 1. Cutting hemp. 2. Mixing hemp with water. 3. Treading the hemp. 4. Making potash from wood. 5. Making a solution from the potash. 6. Straining the mixture. 7. Mixing ash and hemp paste and steaming it. 8 and 9. Pulping the mixture. 10. Stirring mixture in a bath of clean water. 11. Dipping and removing frames from mixture. 12. Drying the frames in the sun.

Above: An hodometer, an instrument for measuring distance travelled by a wheeled vehicle. By means of cogs, after every li (500 metres or 550 yards) travelled one figure strikes the drum; after every ten li travelled the other figure strikes a bell.

Below: A seismograph, an instrument for recording earthquakes, frequent occurrences in China. It was invented by the brilliant Han scientist Chang Heng (AD 78–139). An earthquake tremor causes a vertical pole to tilt against a trigger. This shoots a ball out of the dragon's mouth to the toad below, thus showing the direction of the quake.

Left: Iron-making. Two men operate the huge bellows which raise the temperature in the blast furnaces in which the iron ore is melted. The molten iron then pours into a pan.

SALT FROM THE EARTH

Until the invention of iron, salt could only be made from sea water. With drills made from iron, inland wells as deep as 600 metres (2000 feet) could be bored. Bamboo buckets on long ropes brought the brine (salt-water) up the well. It was then poured into bamboo pipes which carried the water to the stoves, where it was collected in iron pans. The pans were heated over furnaces and the water boiled away leaving salt crystals (a process known as 'evaporation'). This salt was stored in hemp sacks near the fire to keep it dry.

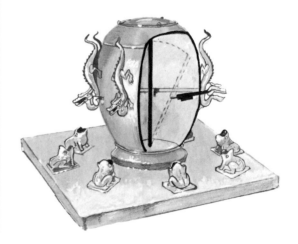

Yang.

Yin

The symbol for Yin and Yang, which the Chinese believed were the two great forces in the world. The two forces were opposites. Yang was positive, male, light and warm; Yin was negative, female, dark and cold. A balance or lack of balance of these forces explained everything that happened in the world.

Lao-tze (above) and Confucius.

Learning and Teaching

After the imperial family, the most respected people in Han China are the scholar-officials. Below them come farmers, followed by craftsmen and finally merchants and soldiers. The scholar-officials run the empire, and all education is directed towards training people for this important task.

Intelligent boys are chosen by officials in the provinces and sent to schools in Loyang. There they learn to read and write. This is very difficult and takes a long time, for in Chinese every word has to be learned individually (unlike most languages in which only the alphabet has to be learned). The students also learn mathematics. But the most important part of their education is studying and learning by heart the teachings of Confucius. This philosopher, or thinker, was born in about 551 BC. He believed in order, respect for people of higher rank, and in setting a good example. His golden rule was: 'Do not do to others what you do not want done to you'. In his books you could read short poems and stories; but Confucius did not think up everything that he wrote. Sometimes he would put in a story that some passing traveller had told him.

Any student who does well enough at school and who is considered honest and law-abiding is sent to court for a trial period. If he passes, he may be made an official.

In later dynasties, applicants had to sit several stiff written examinations. The British system for entry into the civil service is copied from the Chinese.

TWO GREAT THINKERS

The Chinese have never had one religion or a single god in which everyone believed. In the early days they worshipped a number of different nature gods and spirits. They believed that everything in nature, particularly such things as mountains, rivers, and winds, had spirits in them. The emperor was go-between for earth and heaven. He offered sacrifices – sometimes human ones – to the spirits so that they would be kind.

The people of the Han empire still believed in these nature gods, but they also followed the teachings of such great teachers as the Buddha (see page 23), Confucius and Lao-tze. Lao-tze and Confucius both lived at about the same time (551 BC–479 BC). Confucius believed that the perfect ruler, one who believed in order and rank, would govern by example. People would so admire him that there would be no need for laws.

Lao-tze's philosophy, Taoism (pronounced Dowism) is very different. Lao-tze taught that the 'way' to live cannot be described. People should live by the 'principle of nature' and not try to order the world with fixed ideas of what is right and wrong. Some later Taoist masters claimed that they could prolong life for ever. This search for eternal life became a popular cult and several emperors were fooled into believing such claims.

The Taoists have hundreds of gods, ranging from the god of wealth to the god of the kitchen!

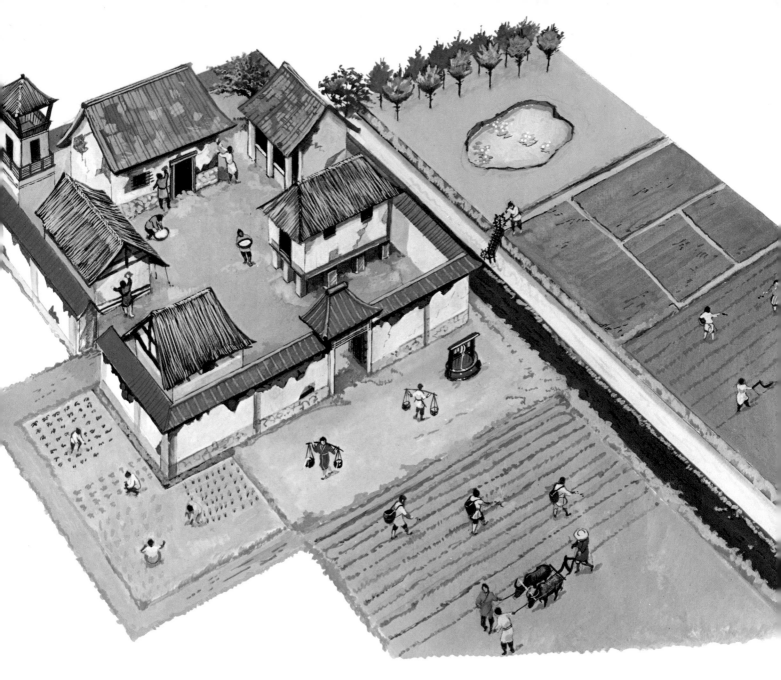

Working the Land

Peasant farmers, however poor, had always been highly respected in China. During the Shang and Chou dynasties the peasant had worked for the large landowners, but by the Han dynasty peasants are farming their own land.

The food for Loyang is produced by peasant farmers who live in riverside villages or homesteads outside the town. The illustration above shows a busy springtime scene in a typical homestead. Houses in the villages are sometimes two-storied and have either thatched or tiled roofs. (We know this from earthenware models that have been found in tombs.)

The soil that the farmers till is yellow. In Chinese it is called *huang-t'u* ('yellow earth'). This loess, as we call it, is formed by sand and dust blown by the wind from the deserts of north-east China.

A springtime scene on a farm. It is time for ploughing and sowing. To irrigate the land water is raised from the well in buckets and carried on a pole. A more advanced method is the irrigation machine (which you can see in the picture). The machine consists of a chain of scoops operated by pedals. As they turn, the scoops lift water from the pond to the irrigation canals along the fields. Spring is also the time when houses are re-plastered and painted.

13

The Farmer's Year

The main crops in northern China are wheat, millet and hemp. In the south the main crop is rice.

In spring the fields are ploughed by ox-drawn ploughs with iron-tipped shares; sometimes the old type of wooden hand-pushed plough is used. The furrows are then sown with crops and vegetables such as leeks, garlic and cabbages. Lac trees, a type of oak from which lacquer is made, are planted at this time too.

Hemp is harvested in late May. Most people's clothes are made of hemp and its seeds can be eaten when millet is scarce. It grows to over two metres (six feet) tall. It is softened by soaking, a process called 'retting', and dried in the sun before the fibre can be separated from the woody stem. The woody stem is used as fuel.

Later in the summer, while the men are hoeing and tending the crops, the women are making silk. The silk comes from moth caterpillars that feed on mulberry leaves.

In autumn the harvest is reaped with iron sickles and taken to the granary. The granary is raised on stilts to keep out the damp and rats. The grain is first separated from the husks by threshing. One method uses a treadle which is a simple lever worked by the foot. The 'pestle' hammer drops down when the foot is raised and so pounds the grain. The

Summer on the farm. The peasants are hoeing a field of half-grown millet. Some of the women are busy spinning and weaving silk. It is the women's job to look after the silk worms and to feed them on mulberry leaves. For many hundreds of years the Chinese were the only people who knew how silk is made. Terrible punishments were threatened for anyone who told foreigners the secret of the silk worm.

grain is then separated from the chaff, or winnowed. The grain may be milled (turned into flour) with a rotary hand mill. This consists of two interlocking furrowed stones. Grain is poured in through a hole in the top and ground between the rotating stones.

In winter the farmer rests and mends his equipment for the next season. If he has suffered from drought, flood or a poor harvest, he may have to sell everything to pay his taxes and work for someone else.

Each year every male between the age of 23 and 56 has to spend a month working for the emperor. He may have to work on the canals, the Great Wall or in an iron or salt mine.

Above: In autumn the men gather the harvest in buckets and wheelbarrows, and take it to the granary. The women are washing, mending and making clothes.

Below: Winter is the time for making and mending tools, and for resting. But for some it is time to serve a period of labour for the state. You can see them being marched off by officials.

15

The Market Place

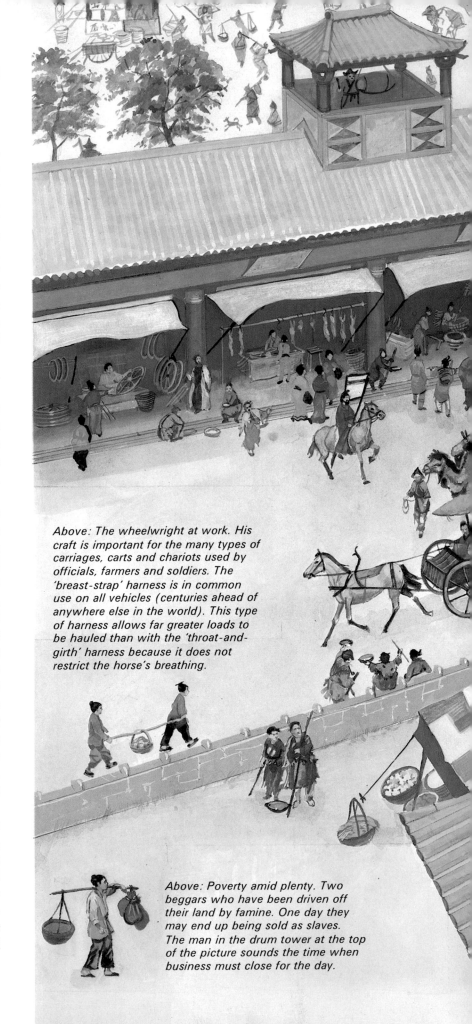

Unlike farmers, merchants are much despised. It is thought shameful to make money from other people, instead of making an honest living from the land. In order to restrict their power the merchants are forbidden to take official posts, and are not allowed to wear silk clothes. Nonetheless many of the merchants of Loyang are very rich, because the market trade is an essential part of town life and has to cater for the needs of the 200,000 people living in the town.

In the market places near the main gates a lively trade is carried on. Through the main gate people are unloading goods from boats on the river. As well as traders from the surrounding countryside there are foreign merchants who have travelled by camel from central Asia.

Near the wall of the market place itself stand two officials who supervise the trading and collect taxes in grain or cash from the stall-holders. All kinds of goods are sold from the stalls – fruit and vegetables, cooked meats, pots and pans, and fine cloths and jewellery. In the market square there is also a public scribe who writes letters or documents for people who cannot write. In the shade of the tree a small group has gathered round a story-teller. One of the most popular people is the soup-seller. As he goes from town to town selling his soup, he passes on local news and gossip. Occasionally there is the gruesome spectacle of a public hanging.

Many luxuries from distant lands are on sale in the market – glass, precious stones, gold and silver from Rome, furs and jade from central Asia. In exchange the foreign merchants return home laden with sumptuous Chinese silks. The gates to the market place are closed at nightfall and re-open at dawn.

Above: The wheelwright at work. His craft is important for the many types of carriages, carts and chariots used by officials, farmers and soldiers. The 'breast-strap' harness is in common use on all vehicles (centuries ahead of anywhere else in the world). This type of harness allows far greater loads to be hauled than with the 'throat-and-girth' harness because it does not restrict the horse's breathing.

Above: Poverty amid plenty. Two beggars who have been driven off their land by famine. One day they may end up being sold as slaves. The man in the drum tower at the top of the picture sounds the time when business must close for the day.

Above: The market places are near the main gates and are surrounded by walls. As well as the strident calls of stallholders hawking their wares can be heard the squawks of a cockfight and the solemn tones of a Buddhist teacher telling a group of people about a new religion from India.

Pleasures and Pastimes

The rich people of Loyang spend a great deal of time relaxing and enjoying themselves.

The rich household in the picture on the right has its own troupe of dancers, as well as jesters, acrobats, jugglers and its own small orchestra. The instruments of the orchestra include pan-pipes, called *sheng*, flat stringed instruments, called *ch'in*, drums and beautiful bronze bells which hang on a frame and are struck with a stick. The dancing girls wear colourful, patterned robes. Their hands are covered by long sleeves which flow gracefully as they move.

Most people love to gamble. In one corner a group of people is watching a cock-fight. Bets have been laid on the winner. Bull-fights are also popular; so too are fights between man and bull. And soldiers often amuse themselves by attaching horns to their heads and having butting contests.

Near the house a group of people is playing a board game called *liu-po* or 'sixes'. Six bamboo sticks with various markings on them are shaken and thrown out of a cup. How they land determines where the player moves his counter on the board. Large sums of money can be won or lost at this game.

Flying kites is another popular pastime. Kites were invented in China – mainly for military purposes to send messages. One general of the Han period flew a kite over his enemy's camp and used the cord to measure the length of the tunnel his troops would have to dig in order to reach it.

Below: A model of acrobats entertaining courtiers. It is from models such as these that we know the type of thing people liked to watch and play at in those days.

Outside the house a couple play liu-po *while dancers, knife-throwers and musicians perform in the courtyard for a few important officials. In the corner cocks are set to fight and bets are laid on the winner.*

Huntsmen set off for the hills in search of deer and wild boar. The emperor has his own hunting parks. His retinue follow him in carriages and on horseback. Imperial huntsmen sport special hats decorated with pheasants' tails and wear trousers of white tiger skin. Drums are beaten to flush out leopards, panthers, wolves and bears.

The poor man trudging home laden with firewood knows little of the pleasures of the big house which the cock-seller has just left.

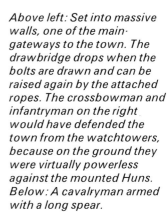

Defending the Empire

Loyang and other towns of the Han empire are protected from enemy attack by a strong system of defences. Surrounding Loyang itself is a thick wall and a moat. At the first signal of danger the massive gates to the town are closed and the moatbridge removed. From the multi-storey watch-towers, troops prepare to shower the attackers with spears and arrows from their crossbows.

The empire's principal line of defence against foreign invasion is the mighty 2400-kilometre (1500-mile) long Great Wall that stretches along the northern frontiers. In earlier times individual states had built walls along their northern borders to stop repeated invasion from the *Hsiung-nu*, or Huns, a nomadic people to the north and north-west, who lived by herding and hunting. In times of drought or famine the Huns would ride south to pillage food. Unlike the Han people, they were superb horsemen and so the Chinese would try to bribe them with gifts of silk; on one occasion they even sent

Above left: Set into massive walls, one of the main gateways to the town. The drawbridge drops when the bolts are drawn and can be raised again by the attached ropes. The crossbowman and infantryman on the right would have defended the town from the watchtowers, because on the ground they were virtually powerless against the mounted Huns. Below: A cavalryman armed with a long spear.

beautiful princesses as wives for their leaders. But at the start of the Ch'in dynasty in 221 BC the emperor ordered thousands of workers to join up the already existing sections of wall. In this way the Great Wall was created. Also at about this time the cross-bow was invented. This had a longer range than the Huns' longbows, so that the Chinese were now able to beat them.

Most able-bodied men from Loyang and other cities must spend two years in the army. They receive no pay, but are given food rations, clothing and equipment. The newly enlisted soldiers may be sent to crush a rebellion somewhere in the empire, or they may be ordered on a campaign of conquest to the south or south east, or to Korea in the north.

Other enlisted men do garrison duty along the Great Wall. The route march from Loyang takes several weeks. Once there the guards have to endure the freezing northern winters, far harsher than the mild climate of Loyang. When not on guard duty, the soldiers are kept busy repairing and improving the wall and the watchtowers in which they are billeted.

This flying horse statue, with its flared nostrils and powerful stride, reflects the awe and admiration the Chinese felt for horses. At first they only had small ponies, but during an invasion they captured some strong, swift Ferghana horses. On these 'celestial' or 'blood sweating' mounts the heavily armed Chinese soldiers were a match for the invading Huns.

A section of the Great Wall winds its way into the distance. Thousands of slaves and unpaid workers died during its construction.

Burial Customs

In the Shang dynasty, when a king or a member of royalty died, horses and chariots were driven into the grave and slaves and attendants were buried with them. By the Han dynasty, this cruel custom had stopped.

The picture above shows the tomb of Prince Liu Sheng, son of the Han Emperor Ching (157 BC–147 BC). The tomb was discovered in 1968 by soldiers of the People's Liberation Army. In the rear chamber his body lies encased in a beautiful jade suit. The suit is made of 2498 carefully shaped pieces of jade, held together with knots of gold wire. Near the body are sacrificial objects, also made of jade. In the tomb, too, are beautiful bronze vessels and lamps inlaid with gold and silver. In other chambers are buried pottery models of houses, farmyards, animals, cooking stoves and figures of attendants and entertainers. There are pots of wine and food, complete

A reconstruction of the tomb in which Prince Liu Sheng, encased in a jade suit, was buried His wife, Tou Wan, was buried in a similar tomb. Both tombs were hollowed out of the solid rock and filled with huge amounts of treasure and playthings for the dead persons' use in the after-life.

with chopsticks, and even the Prince's chariots and horses. Everything in the tomb is for his use in after-life.

Death in China was surrounded by all sorts of ceremonies. Everything possible was done to see the dead safely into the next world. The funerals of the rich were very elaborate. Most important was to find the right place for the grave, for it was essential not to upset the earth spirits. If the grave was sited in the wrong spot, bad luck could befall the family.

Huge amounts of money were spent on funerals by those who wished to gain prestige by showing devotion to their parents. The lacquered coffins were placed in a brick vault cut deep into the earth. A mound of earth or shrine would be built on top. The poor could not afford such extravagant funerals and were buried in pits or simple coffins.

Above: In 1968 two ancient tombs were found in western China. They belonged to Prince Liu Sheng and his wife Tou Wan, who were buried in the 2nd century BC. The tombs had been hollowed out of solid rock, each consisting of several huge chambers filled with treasures.

These Buddhist statues, near Loyang, were carved out of the cliffs. Each of them is about 15 metres (50 feet) high. You can see the caves dug by Buddhists and which were used as places in which to meditate.

BUDDHISM

Buddhism, one of the world's great religions, reached China from India in about AD 60, during the Han dynasty. At first the Buddhist community in Loyang were mainly foreigners and merchants who had been converted abroad.

Buddhists believe that after you die, you are reborn. If you have led a bad life, you will be reborn in a 'lower state' – perhaps as an ant! By giving up 'desires', you can escape this rebirth cycle and eventually reach the state of *nirvana* or paradise where you remain for ever.

Right: An ornamental brick depicting the gateway to a grand house, with guards and a garden beyond. It was found in a tomb dating from the Han period.

Overleaf: A painting on silk from a scroll called 'Admonitions of the Instructress to the Court Ladies'. The lady on the right is writing on a scroll.

IMPORTANT HAPPENINGS

	China	Asia
BC 3500	*c*3500-1500 New Stone Age. First advanced human beings inhabit Yellow River basin. They had learned to decorate pots and cut and polish stone. *c*2000-1500 Legendary Hsia Dynasty. *c*1500-1027 Shang Dynasty arises. Bronze Age. First organized society. Anyang becomes capital. *c*1027-771 Shang defeated by Chou who came from a province north-west of Loyang; Western Chou Dynasty. *c*722-256 Eastern Chou Dynasty. The dynasty is divided into two periods: *c*722-481 The Spring and Autumn period. Confucius (born 551) and Lao-tze (born 640) live in this time. *c*600 First ironworking.	*c*2500 Indus Valley civilization arises in India. *c*1750 Break-up of Indus Valley civilization. *c*1500 Indus Valley civilization falls to invaders. *c*660 Jimmu Tenno, legendary first emperor of Japan, accedes. *c*600 Early cities around river Ganges, India. 563 The Buddha born in Nepal, India. 533 Persians invade India, by now highly civilized with towns, cities and extensive overseas trade. North-west India becomes a province of Persian Empire for 200 years. Introduction of Persian art and religion.
BC 500	481-221 The Warring States period. The ruling state of Chou is weak and the seven largest states fight among themselves, until the Ch'in defeats them all and unites the empire. 221-206 The Ch'in Dynasty. Weights, measures and writing are standardized. 213 Emperor Huang Ti orders 'Burning of the Books'. All books but those on practical subjects are burned. *c*210 The Great Wall completed; Silk Road to Europe established. Death of Huang Ti. 206 Western Han Dynasty begins with peasant leader Liu Pang who becomes Emperor (to 195 BC). 141-87 Rule of Emperor Wu ti—regarded as the peak of Han power. His generals expand the empire in all directions conquering Manchuria, Korea and southern China. They make contact with Vietnam, India and Rome.	327 Alexander the Great invades north India. 305 Chandragupta drives Greeks from India; founds Mauryan Empire. 274-237 Emperor Ashoka reigns in India. Buddhism becomes widespread. *c*185-AD 320 Invaders (Asiatic Greeks, Scythians, Parthians and Kushans) settle in north India and Punjab.
AD 9	9-23 Wang Mang proclaims his own dynasty, the 'Hsin'. He fails and peasant rebellions arise led by the 'Red Eyebrows' who are loyal to the Han family. 25-220 Eastern Han: Kuang-wu restores the dynasty. Confucianism and Civil Service established. Accurate calendar. First national library. Astronomers predict eclipses. Invention of paper, lacquer and the sundial. *c*60 The entry of Buddhism into China from India. 92-192 Period of decline; the imperial family and national army become more powerful than the emperor. 184 Popular rebellions break out. The rebels are known as 'The Yellow Turbans'. *c*220-265 The Three Kingdoms. Three Han generals divide the empire among themselves. 265-581 Long period of disunity called the 'Six Dynasties', poetry and painting continue to flourish. 581-618 The empire is united under the Sui Dynasty, with the capital at Ch'angan. They build the first Grand Canal linking the Yangtze with the Yellow River.	200-700 Great Tombs period in Japan. 360-390 Japanese empress Jingo sends troops to Korea.
AD 907	618-907 T'ang Dynasty founded by Li Yuan. Under the T'ang, Chinese civilization reaches its highest point.	712 Oldest Japanese historical text—the Kojiki is written.

Europe and Near East	Northern Europe	
c3100 First writing in Mesopotamia. First Egyptian Dynasty.	c3000 New Stone Age in northern Europe. c1800-1400 Stonehenge built in Britain (2nd–3rd phase).	**BC 3500**
c3000-1500 The Minoans flourish on Crete. c2686-2181 Egypt's Old Kingdom. c2600-2400 Royal Graves of Ur. c2372-2255 Akkadian Empire founded by Sargon in Sumeria. c2050-1786 Egypt's Middle Kingdom.	c1500-1300 Bronze Age.	
c1800-1750 Hammurabi rules Babylon. Horses trained to pull carts.	c700 Halstatt culture—first use of iron.	
c1600-1200 Mycenaean civilization flourishes in Greece. c1567-1085 Egypt's New Kingdom. c1450 Cretan civilization destroyed. Hittite Empire at its height (to 1180 BC). c1420-1385 Golden Age of Egypt. c1200-800 Collapse of Mycenaean civilization. c1200 Sea Peoples raid Mediterranean coasts. Siege of Troy. Hebrews occupy Canaan.	c450 Celtic La Tène culture develops.	**BC 500**
1150 Greeks begin to colonize coast of Asia Minor. Rise of Phoenician sea-power. c1100 Phoenician colonies in Spain. 1085-333 Egypt's late Dynastic Period. 973 Solomon becomes King of Israel. c900 Rise of Etruscans in Italy. 850-650 Rise of Greek city-states. 776 Traditional date of first Olympic Games. 705-682 Sennacherib becomes King of Assyria and establishes his capital at Nineveh (701). 670 Assyrians invade Egypt. 612 Medes and allies overthrow Assyrian Empire.		
605-561 Nebuchadnezzar II rules Babylon. 586 Nebuchadnezzar besieges Jerusalem. 539 Cyrus of Persia conquers Babylonia. 525 Persians invade Egypt. 510 Founding of Roman Republic. 508 Athenian democracy begins. 486-465 King Xerxes rules the Persian Empire. 460-429 Age of Pericles in Athens. 431-404 Peloponnesian War. Athens surrenders to Spartans. 334-390 Conquests of Alexander the Great. 323 Alexander dies. End of Great Age of Greece. 281-201 Rome's wars with Carthage. 146 Carthage destroyed.	58-49 Julius Caesar's wars in France and Britain. 9 German barbarians defeat Romans. Roman conquests east of the Rhine are abandoned.	**AD 9**
65-63 Romans conquer Syria and Palestine. 45 Julius Caesar dictator of Rome. 44 Caesar is murdered. 27 Augustus Caesar becomes first Roman emperor.	43 The Romans invade Britain. 61 Boudicca's (Boadicea) rebellion in eastern Britain is put down.	
4 Probably date of birth of Jesus Christ. c30 Crucifixion of Jesus Christ. 98-117 Emperor Trajan extends Roman Empire to its greatest extent. 286 Roman Empire divided into Western and Eastern Empires. 330 Founding of Constantinople as new capital of Roman Empire. 476 Fall of Rome: Goths force last emperor to abdicate. 570 Muhammad born at Mecca.	101-107 Trajan's wars in Dacia (Romania). 122 Hadrian's wall across northern Britain commenced. 270-275 Goths take Dacia (central Europe). 284-305 Diocletian checks Rome's decline. 407 Last Roman troops withdrawn from Britain. 432 Mission of St Patrick to Ireland. 449 Jutes under Hengist and Horsa invade Britain. 451 Attila the Hun invades Gaul; defeated by Franks and Romans at Chalons. 800 Charlemagne crowned as Holy Roman Emperor.	**AD 907**

GLOSSARY OF TERMS

Ancestor worship Until modern times, the Chinese honoured and revered dead members of their families. The dead were treated as if they were still alive: no important decision could be taken without consulting them.

Anyang City in Honan province, eastern China, near to the site of the Shang capital of *c*1300 BC, where many Oracle Bones were discovered during excavations of royal tombs.

Bean-curd Smooth purée of soya beans which is pressed into cakes.

Brine A mixture of salt and water.

Buddha The Buddha ('Enlightened One') was an Indian prince, Siddartha, who lived in the 6th century BC. His ideals of non-violence and respect for life spread rapidly over India and Tibet, reaching China in the 3rd century BC.

Cantonese The main language spoken by the people of South China, named after Canton (Kuang-Chou), the greatest city of the region.

Ch'ang-an Another name for Hsi-an, the ancient capital of the Chinese Empire.

Ch'eng-tu The capital city of Szechwan Province.

Ch'in (pronounced chin) The area of northwest China which, in 221 BC brought all other Chinese states under its rule. The ruler of Ch'in, Shi Huang Ti (259–210 BC), was the first to call himself emperor. In 206 BC, Ch'in fell to the first Han emperor.

Chou (pronounced jo) The dynasty of kings which ruled the feudal states of China from *c*1100–221 BC.

From 771 BC, when the capital was moved to Loyang, the dynasty is called 'Eastern Chou'. It saw the rapid decline of royal power and the rise of semi-independent feudal states.

Cocoon A protective covering of fine thread spun by a caterpillar during the stage at which it is changing into its winged form. Cocoons of silk worms are collected and the thread spun into silk.

Delta Whenever a river enters a large body of water, such as a lake or the sea, it slows down. As a result it drops the sediment it has been carrying, forming a plain of rich soil, called a delta. The delta of the Yellow River has always been one of the most fertile regions of China.

Dragon The serpent-like dragon (lung) played an important part in Chinese myths. It was not always a fearsome beast—in fact, dragons could bring good luck. Dragons could live both in water and in the air—even though they had no wings. The dragon was the symbol of the Chinese royal family and, later, of China itself.

Dynasty A family of rulers. It also means the period during which the line of hereditary rulers ruled.

Edict A proclamation by the government which has the force of law.

Feudal system A type of society in which all land was owned by the ruler. He made grants of land to nobles in return for military service. The land itself was usually worked by landless labourers who, in return, were allowed to keep some of the food they produced.

Fief A stretch of land granted by a Chou king to a noble. In time, the

larger fiefs absorbed small ones and became independent kingdoms.

Gobi The Great Gobi Desert in Mongolia. It is 500–950 kilometres (300–600 miles) wide and 1600 kilometres (1000 miles) long.

Han The name of a dynasty of emperors who ruled China from 202 BC to AD 221. Until AD 6 the Han capital was at Ch'ang-an; after AD 25 it became Loyang.

Hemp A plant with a woody stem that can be split into fibres, used for making rope and twine, as well as fine thread suitable for weaving into cloth. Hempseeds contain a vegetable oil. In ancient times they were used as cattle fodder.

Hokien With Cantonese and Mandarin, one of the three main branches of spoken Chinese.

Hsi Ling Shi The wife of the emperor Huang Ti. In Chinese legend, she discovered how to make silk from the cocoons of the silkworm.

Hsiung-nu Name given by the Chinese to the tribes of 'Northern Barbarians' who lived beyond the Great Wall.

Hsia A dynasty of kings which, according to legend, ruled China before the Shang Dynasty.

Hwang-ho The Chinese name of the great Yellow River—so-called because of the yellow coloured mud which it carries down to the sea.

Jade A very hard stone, green, blue or white in colour.

Keng Stew made from meat or vegetables.

Kung A class of craftsmen in ancient China.

Kowtow The traditional Chinese way of showing great respect to a superior, by kneeling before him and touching one's forehead to the ground.

Lacquer The sap of a kind of oak tree. When heated, the greyish-white treacle turns black. Left in a damp place, it becomes very hard and can be polished until its surface becomes like glass. Pigments can be added.

Li Po Perhaps the most famous Chinese poet, who lived in the 8th century AD and travelled widely through China.

Liu Pang (247–195 BC) A Chinese emperor, the first of the Han Dynasty.

Mandarin The branch of the Chinese language spoken by two-thirds of the people of China. Its Chinese name, kuan-hua, means 'official speech': in imperial times it was the language of the Mandarins, the officials who administered the empire.

Millet A crop like wheat bearing a large number of small nutritious seeds.

Mongolia The name of a huge area of central Asia that was the ancient homeland of the Mongol peoples. It is now divided into Inner Mongolia, part of the People's Republic of China, and Outer Mongolia, part of the USSR.

Neolithic The period (New Stone Age) of shaped, polished tools of stone which preceded bronze working in Shang times.

Nung A class of peasant farmers in ancient China.

Oracle Bones The shoulder blades of oxen, or the lower shells of tortoises; used by ancient Chinese astrol-ogers to foretell the future. Their method was to touch the bone with a red-hot needle, causing the surface to break into a pattern of light cracks. The patterns were examined and interpreted as messages. Some of the earliest examples of Chinese writing have been discovered on oracle bones.

Paper This invention of the early Han period replaced the use of bamboo slips, while introduction of brush and ink revolutionized the speed and style of writing.

Phoenix According to eastern legends, the phoenix was a huge bird with feathers of scarlet and gold. At the end of its long life, it was supposed to set its nest on fire and be swallowed up in the flames. Miraculously, a young phoenix arose from the ashes. In China the phoenix brought prosperity, its departure meant calamity. Artists depicted it with beautiful plumage and a very long tail.

Pictograms A picture which is the symbol for a word.

Pi discs Circular medals of carved jade, pierced with a round hole. They were a symbol of the Supreme Being, Heaven.

Scroll Many Chinese books and paintings were in the form of scrolls—lengths of paper, often mounted on a silk backing, which could be rolled up when not in use.

Shang The despised class of merchants and businessmen in ancient China.

Shang or **Yin** The dynasty which ruled China during the first flowering of Chinese civilization c1500 BC to c1123 BC.

Shih A class of minor nobles and scholars, the most important group of the emperor's subjects.

Sung A dynasty which ruled in China from AD 960 to 1287. There were two Sung periods—the Northern Sung with its capital at Kaifeng, and the Southern Sung, centered on Hangchow. During the Sung period porcelain was made in quantity for the first time.

Sun Wu A famous general of the Chou Dynasty, who wrote a textbook on the science of warfare.

Szechwan A large province in southwest China, famed for its mountains, forests and rivers, the mildness of its climate, and the richness of its soil.

Ts'ui Shi A landowner of the Han period who wrote a famous textbook on farming methods.

Tumuli Mounds of earth built over graves.

Warlords Powerful generals who ruled the provinces at times when the power of the emperor was weak. At various times in Chinese history, struggles between warlords brought great destruction and suffering.

Wu-ti (157–87 BC) The greatest emperor of the Han Dynasty. Under his rule, many new lands were brought into the empire.

Yangtze The greatest river of China and the third longest river in the world. It rises in Tibet and flows for 4900 kilometres (3100 miles) to the Yellow Sea.

Detail of a T'ang Dynasty painting

CHINESE WRITING

an 'oracle' bone

Writing in ancient China was considered an art. The earliest forms of writing were inscriptions scratched on 'oracle' bones used by priests to answer questions. From very early times the writing took the basic form it has today. The system used by the Chinese is based on 'characters' or signs. (It is not an alphabet with signs representing different sounds). Each character stands for a complete idea or thing. The first characters were 'pictograms' – simple drawings of such things as the sun, a house, or a tree. More abstract ideas such as the number 3 could be shown as three straight lines. In time the pictures gradually changed, so that by the Han dynasty almost any object or idea could be put into writing. The illustration (right) shows how a few common characters developed from pictograms. Today Chinese writing has over 70,000 characters, although for practical purposes only a few thousand are needed. This writing system has one great advantage: people who speak Cantonese, Hokien or Mandarin Chinese, while not understanding one another's speech, can read the the same writing. The characters stand for the meaning, rather than the sounds of the words.

The characters above developed from the original pictograms.
The last character shows how an abstract word has been made from two noun pictograms – 'mother' and her 'son'. Combined, the character means both 'to love' and 'good'.

Above: Part of a lacquered wooden screen, from the 5th century AD. On which writing is in two sorts of characters—those used by scribes, and those used by officials. At the bottom an important official is being transported in a sedan chair.

Left: A piece of copper 'cash'. The square hole in the middle is for stringing the coins together. Big business was done using gold ingots, which were worth 10,000 coins each. Some goods were bartered – they changed hands in exchange for other goods.

OTHER BOOKS TO READ

Great Civilizations: Ancient China by Robert Knox (Longman) 1978
A Closer Look at Early China by Wendy Boase (Hamish Hamilton) 1977
China—the land and its people by Jonathan Hammond (Macdonald Educational) 1974
Ancient China by Patrick Fitzgerald (Elsevier Phaidon) 1978
The Treasures and Dynasties of China by Bamber Gascoigne (Jonathan Cape) 1973

INDEX

PHOTOGRAPHIC ACKNOWLEDGEMENTS
The publishers wish to thank the following for supplying photographs for this book: Page 2 William MacQuitty; 9 British Museum; 12 Mansell; 18 Society for Anglo-Chinese Understanding; 21 Zefa; 23 Derek Gillman *left*; Society for Anglo-Chinese Understanding *top*; Michael Holford *bottom*; 24–25 British Museum; 29 William MacQuitty; 30 Society for Anglo-Chinese Understanding *right*; British Museum *left*.